Inaugural Address

of

WILLIAM WESTON PATTON, D. D.,

as

PRESIDENT

of

HOWARD UNIVERSITY.

OCTOBER 9, 1877.

WASHINGTON, D. C.:
W. M. STUART, PRINTER
1877.

INAUGURAL ADDRESS.

The peculiarity of the occasion calls for an appropriate theme, and I therefore invite your attention to The Relation of the Higher Education to a True Civilization, and to the Elevation of a Depressed Race.

A university fully developed, fitly manned, and adequately endowed is the ripest product of modern civilization. It is at once the outgrowth, the sign, and the guaranty of the highest culture of a land. Sending its roots deep into the soil of past generations, and deriving no small part of its vitality from the researches and the renown of scholars who have ceased from earthly studies and gone to wider fields of thought, it also draws to itself the life-giving influences of the air and light of contemporaneous ability and learning. Covering in its various departments, academic training, ancient and modern literature, history, philology, natural science, philosophy, art, medicine, law and theology, it ranges over all the past, while possessing the wide present, and touches human thought and action at every possible point. The name itself stands for the idea of completeness. Hence since the early part of the twelfth century, when the institutions at Bologna and Paris emerge from their obscure beginnings, the names of the universities suggest the course of European history and the glory of their respective lands. Speak to a man of culture of historical France, and by the side of her military fame he will put the renown of her former university of Paris, with its theological college of the Sorbonne, whose doctors at one time decided the grave disputes of all Europe, and feared not to confront and oppose the infallible Pope himself. Name modern Italy, and the universities of Bologna and Padua, of Ferrara and Pisa, of Naples and Palermo, of Perrugia and Parma, with their illustrious compeers, rush at once into thought. Germany—I had almost said, what is it, but the product of the centuries of instructions given within the universities of Heidelberg, Leipsic, Würtzburg, Freiburg, Tübingen, Halle, Göttingen, and more modern institutions? The influential thinking of Great Britain has been done by the men trained at Cambridge and Oxford, at St. Andrews, Aberdeen, and Edinburgh. While our own land has had little but the superabounding name of university, having developed in the place gymnasia, under the title of colleges, yet these, with the higher professional schools, have not been a wholly inadequate substitute, and throughout our brief history they have furnished a large proportion of the men who have shaped and administered our national affairs. By the necessity of the case, a university, with its several co-ordinate faculties under a common organization, implies variety of knowledge with unity of object, or wide and increasing learning devoted to the advancement of country and mankind. It could exist only as it fell heir to the treasures of the buried past; it could have a right to continue to be, only as it sought to transmit these, with all possible enrichment, to the fast-coming future, and to use them in uplifting the race from the limitations and degradations of ignorance. Slow of growth is such an institution, and it must draw its resources from many quarters, making friends of all lovers of humanity, rejoicing in the smile of the State, and privileged with the blessing of the Church.

In the Old World such institutions received their earliest inspiration from the Church, springing from the scholastic discussions of the middle ages; but they have also owed their prosperity largely to the State, which gave them incorporation and revenues, and retained a quite positive control. It was the glory of a king or emperor, to found a university and to build a cathedral. In this New World, the higher institutions of learning have principally sprung from and been supported by private generosity, receiving from the State simply legal recognition in the form of a charter, with an occasional gift of money or land. It is thus that the colleges of New England and of the Middle States were established. The plan of a State University, under direct legislative control, and supported by the public treasury, which has been attempted at the South and West, has been a noticeable success in but a single instance, and then at the expense of much personal and political contention. The preference for private control has arisen from a general jealousy of the State, and from the American principle of separating it from everything which concerns religion. A true university must embrace a department of Theology—a fact which, under our American system, at once cuts it off from State support and control, or compels it to exist in a mutilated condition, which belies its name; as if a sculptor should carve from the marble an Apollo lacking a limb, or, I might rather say, lacking a head! Not only so, but it may be predicted that, in the progress of philosophic, scientific, and theologic discussion, as lines shall be more narrowly drawn, and as differing consciences shall come into action, State Universities will find themselves in trouble, even without a theological department; for religion must be taught, or implied, or denied, in all the higher education; because its principles run everywhither, and touch human thought and life universally. It is simply impossible to impart a knowledge of philosophy, or history, or classical literature, or modern literature, as these should be studied in university-courses, and in the spirit of a true scholarship, without canvassing points which involve religious differences, as between denominations of Christians, especially Protestants and Romanists, and as between Christians and the deniers of a supernatural religion. To preserve logical consistency and to avoid serious practical difficulty, it would appear necessary for the State ultimately to withdraw entirely from the field of the higher education, and to confine itself to the secularized common school system for imparting to the masses a knowledge of the needful primary branches.

But the complete university-training is essential to the development of any race and nation, and must be a factor in the highest civilization. Every people grows *to* it when rising from barbarism, and then grows *by* it in the development of the national life. Hence we not only note that the progress of the civilization of modern Europe and that of its universities is a parallel progress, but that, at a certain stage of the advancement of all races, whom we are striving to elevate, the demand is inevitably made for the establishment of institutions for the higher education. This is found to be necessary to give permanence to the lower stages, as well as to continue the upward movement. Hence, where Christian missions have reached a sufficient development, they found a college, as a natural result. The American Board of Commissioners for Foreign Missions have seen five such institutions grow up on their field within twenty years; which will soon be followed by as many more, till amid the benighted races a Christian civilization shall be established upon a firm basis. For every such institution is both reservoir and fountain. It collects from surrounding springs of thought and science whatever tends to human elevation, and it diffuses this by numberless streams through all classes of society. It is easy and instructive to trace this relation of the University to the development and elevation of the people, which, however, we can do but briefly at this time.

First of all, it establishes the standard of national culture. The " high-water mark" of intellectual advancement is fixed by the university-education, which thus measures and defines the civilization of the people. There are distinct types of mental culture, which are represented by the *literati* of the various lands, who have their respective standards of learning. Compare, in this respect, the higher education of the Chinese, of the Mohammedan nations, and of Europe. Each represents a marked advance of the human mind, under such masters as Confucius, Mohammed and Jesus; and in each case the special form of civilization has crystalized in the superior schools or colleges. Hence China never thinks of a progress beyond that attained three thousand years since, as its results are taught in the colleges now maintained in the large cities. In like manner the schools or colleges of the Softas fix the limit of Mohammedan culture. And even under our own civilization a peculiar stamp is given to the mind of the individual student and to the conceptions of culture generally entertained, according as the prevailing character of the university-education is Christian or Rationalistic, is Protestant or Romish. In the university is the fountain-head, higher than which the streams will not rise. Scholarship means acquiring what is there taught. Learning signifies eminent acquisitions in the branches of study there recognized. Thus the difference in the universities of various lands marks their standards of scholarly culture, which we know to differ precisely in this way, in America, in Great Britain, and in Germany.

Next we observe, that these crowning institutions of education excite the enthusiasm and stir the ambition of the best youthful minds among a people. They do a double work—of selection and of training. The selection is of the natural or Darwinian sort. No explorers are sent forth to ascertain who among the youth have genius and aspiration, and to invite or command their attendance within university walls. It is not as when the eye discovers, and the hand grasps, diamonds among pebbles; but rather as when the magnet comes in contact with the sand, and draws to itself the kindred particles. A university exists and does its work in a land, and there are attracted to it, as by a necessity of their nature, the minds that thirst for knowledge and that aim at the distinctions known to depend upon knowledge. It is in this well-known effect, of suggestion and inspiration, that at least a partial compensation has been found for the unwise multiplication of colleges in our land. They have doubled the number of those who otherwise would have sought a liberal education. By them the appeal in favor of learning has been brought home to every considerable community, urban or rural, by the impressiveness of the buildings, by the sight of the professors and students, by the new topics of conversation and discussion, and by the influence of the commencement occasions and of other public literary exercises. Each has interested a wide circle of friends, on local, reformatory, or denominational grounds, has secured endowed scholarships, and has carried the inspiring idea of a possible liberal education down among the people and before the mind of every mechanic's and farmer's boy. Hence come deep and unexpected thoughts, the kindling of noble ambitions, and the rousing of latent powers, resulting in heroic, self-denying effort and triumphant accomplishment.

In these institutions also is gained the needed preparation for achieving the highest results in each grand department of life and work. The preparation is both specific and general. The university-education, in the American form, fits specifically for each calling of civilized life in which knowledge and culture and professional acquirements are the conditions of success. To enumerate such departments as the Classical and Scientific Courses, and those of Theology, Philosophy, Medicine, Law and Art, is to represent the leading forces in the politics, literature, religion, science and industry of the world. Hence from the universities will largely come the erudite scholars, the eminent authors, the explorers and discoverers in new fields of thought, the able and accomplished editors, the broad-minded statesmen, the skillful physicians and surgeons, the able instructors, the eloquent preachers, the competent advocates and judges. Such must have the advantages which a university offers, would they attain to the highest success and fill the entire circle of their responsibilities; for thus alone can they be thoroughly grounded in the principles and details of their respective professions.

But the general preparation is equally important, as found in the severe intellectual discipline and in the broad literary culture which result from the university-training, and which, aside from professional details, afford that grasp of mind, solidity of judgment, readiness of faculty, concentration of thought, freedom from prejudice, and love of truth and beauty, which fit a man for all possible work. This is the result usually least appreciated, and yet widest in its bearings. Lord Macaulay gave an admirable illustration of its practical bearings, in his discussion of Civil Service Reform, and of Competitive Examinations. In his report he said:

"Skill in Greek and Latin versification has, indeed, no direct tendency to form a judge, a financier, or a diplomatist; but the youth who does best what all the ablest and most ambitious youths about him are trying to do well, will generally prove a superior man: nor can we doubt that an accomplishment by which Fox and Canning, Greenville and Wellesley, Mansfield and Tenterden first distinguished themselves above their fellows indicates powers of mind which, properly trained and directed, may do great service to the State."

So important is his testimony as to the practical character of a liberal education in fitting for official duties of every kind, that I venture on more extended extracts from his speech in 1833 on East India Company's Charter Bill:

"It is proposed that for every vacancy in the civil service four candidates shall be named, and the candidate elected by examination. We conceive that under this system the persons sent out will be young men above par—young men superior either in talents or in diligence to the mass. It is said, I know, that examinations in Latin, in Greek, and in mathematics are no tests of what men will prove to be in life. I am perfectly aware that they are not infallible tests, but that they are tests I confidently maintain. Look at every walk of life—at this house: at the other house; at the bar; at the bench; at the church—and see whether it be not true that those who attain high distinction in the world are generally men who are distinguished in their academic career. Indeed, sir, this objection would prove far too much, even for those who use it. It would prove that there is no use at all in education. Why should we put boys out of their way? Why should we force a lad, who would much rather fly a kite or trundle a hoop, to learn his Latin grammar? Why should we keep a young man to his Thucydides or his Laplace, when he would rather be shooting? Education would be mere useless torture if, at two or three and twenty, a man who has neglected his studies were exactly on a par with a man who has applied himself to them—exactly or likely to perform all the offices of public life with credit to himself and with advantage to society. Whether the English system of education be good or bad is not now the question. Perhaps I may think that too much time is given to the ancient languages and to the abstract sciences. But what then? Whatever be the languages, whatever be the sciences which it is in any age and country the fashion to teach, those who become the greatest proficients in those languages and those sciences will generally be the flower of the youth—the most acute, the most industrious, the most ambitious of honorable distinctions. If the Ptolemaic system were taught at Cambridge instead of the Newtonian, the 'Senior Wrangler' would nevertheless be in general a superior man to the 'Wooden Spoon.' If instead of learning Greek, we learned the Cherokee, the man who understood the Cherokee best, who made the most correct and melodious Cherokee verses, who comprehended most accurately the effect of the Cherokee particles, would generally be a superior man to him who was destitute of these accomplishments. If Astrology were taught at our universities, the young man who cast nativities best would generally turn out a superior man. If Alchemy were taught, the young man who showed the most activity in the pursuit of the philosopher's stone would generally turn out a superior man."—*Speeches I, 267, &c.*

These are not only the words of a scholar and a statesman, but they appeal to the common sense of every man.

Further, it should be considered that the university-influence ultimately tends to elevate the ideas and guide the action of

2

the mass of the people. Thought is like water, which spreads in every direction upon the earth, sinks into every crevice of the rock, and even moistens the air above. The ideas of the university color, in time, the thinking of the masses. Thus, recently in Germany and France, during an age of scholarly unbelief, skepticism and rationalism have come to leaven the entire nation. Materialism in the philosopher issues as Communism in the citizen. But if error in such institutions proves pervasive, so does truth; and the reason that, in our own land, the popular mind thus far has sustained evangelical religion, and also, on the whole, wise and righteous measures of civil government, is found in the extent of liberal education from the beginning, by which a high average intelligence has been preserved. Out of the university come the superior teachers for the various grades of schools, as also the leaders of thought and action around whom the people rally, in Church and in State. For in both of these relations the people will have leaders; and if these cannot be provided through educated men in the various professions and business callings, they will be found in ignorant and ambitious men among themselves, or in the unscrupulous demagogues of a class slightly above them. A thoughtful observer must have felt, during the recent strikes and riots, that one great need of working men is, to be kept in contact with the intelligence and virtue of the upper classes, to partake of their ideas and principles, and to receive leaders of more honesty and wisdom, who shall have a conception of the solidarity of interests in a community. It requires intelligence to have, in the proper sense of the word, a commonwealth; for unity of aim and effort is always made impossible by ignorance, which, in its suspicion and fear, in its narrow vision and sudden impulse, fails to recognize those great principles which necessitate common action, and those true friends who seek broad results and a permanent welfare.

But it is time for me to pass from these general considerations to their more particular connection with the occasion which has convened this intelligent audience.

Howard University has, in one respect, but a slender claim

to represent the fact and influence of University-Education. Being at the beginning of its career, with resources confessedly small, pecuniarily and otherwise, an unfriendly critic might suggest that, as with many other American institutions, its name is the grandest thing about it. Doubtless, also, others, who look with a prejudiced eye upon its thoroughly democratic basis of giving equal educational advantages to all, irrespective of race or sex, and its special encouragement of the race which hitherto has been largely excluded from literary institutions, will indulge in a sneer of contempt for its object, or in an exclamation of incredulity as to its success. Nevertheless it proposes to bear its part in the noble work of human elevation, which has been briefly outlined, and its friends have faith to believe that its object will justify itself to every patriot and Christian. Howard University is a child of Providence, and an heir of the new future, born out of the great civil war, which, in saving the National Union, gave freedom to four millions of slaves. That, be it remembered, was an emancipation of four millions of minds, as well as of so many bodies. The greatest crime of slavery was its virtual annihilation of the minds of its victims. Hence, freedom instantly created a demand for an immense addition to the educational instrumentalities of the land, of every grade—for the common school, the high school, the college, and the professional seminary; that the new citizens might be fitted to assume their responsible position, and to fill every post to which they might be called, from the lowest to the highest. With a wise forecast it was determined to locate at the Nation's Capital a University, which should be open, in all departments, to young men and young women of every race and color, upon equal terms. For what has learning to do with distinctions of race or complexion? Is knowledge Caucasian, or Mongolian, or African? Is literature white, red, yellow, or black? Surely science, as such, has to do with mind, not with varieties of race; with man, not merely with the white man. Every true friend of learning takes as his motto that famous sentiment of the ancient poet, Terence, who was by birth an African and by position a freedman: "*Homo sum, et nil humani a me alienum puto*"—"I am a man, and count nothing that is human foreign to me." In this spirit Howard University opens its doors to all comers who thirst for knowledge. And if Dartmouth College, now of honorable and wide repute, began but as a humble school for the North American Indian, there may be a glorious future for this institution, which, excluding none, yet has a word of special encouragement for the non-Caucasian races. The value of such an institution in aiding to solve a national problem, and to meet the pressing wants of millions hitherto in the most depressed condition of humanity, will be more evident if we bear in mind certain considerations which often are overlooked.

First of all, it must never be forgotten by the colored people, or by their friends, that they can be elevated upon no principles and by no instrumentalities other than those which apply to mankind in general. As "there is no royal road to learning" to suit dullards of kingly birth, so no peculiar and accommodating pathway to wealth and power, to civilization and culture, opens before those of African descent. Their own expectations and the efforts of those who would assist them must be based simply on their manhood. It is only as this shall be developed and brought to bear upon life's duties and opportunities, that progress can be made in outward condition and in the estimation of mankind. There are no sudden results to be secured by artificial means. Neither special legislation, nor military protection, nor favor extended by those in power, nor the peculiar regard and effort of philanthropists will, of themselves, avail to procure the abolition of caste-feeling, and the elevation of the colored people to an entire equality with the whites. The effects of ages of slavery are not to be removed in a day, by a mere legislative vote. An amendment to the Constitution alters no fact of ignorance, of poverty, of moral debasement. The prejudices of the whites, descending through generations, imbibed by individuals in infancy and strengthened by universal sentiment, practice, and association of ideas, cannot be easily and soon overcome, and are not, so far as feeling is concerned, wholly within the power of volition, so as to be annihilated at will. They will vanish gradually in the presence of increasing evidence of a noble manhood. Developed intellectual power, the higher education, success in industrial pursuits, the acquirement of wealth and culture and character, will cause it to disappear as the sun does the heavy, chilly, obscuring mists which night generates in the valleys. When I deposit a gold coin on the table, it commands a certain degree of respect. No one is obliged to argue in its behalf. It speaks for itself. Having intrinsic value and the added stamp of the national mint, it represents so many grains of precious metal and their equivalent in whatever money will buy. Hence everybody welcomes it, and looks upon it with regard. Will the result not be analogous, when the colored man shall be seen to have an intrinsic value equal to that of the white man? When one shall no longer associate with him the ideas of bondage, pauperism, and barbarism, but those of freedom, prosperity, intelligence, and culture? When he shall not only carry in his person the stamp of American citizenship, but shall come out from a university-training a scholar and a gentleman, like a glittering coin from the die?

But in securing this result, so difficult and yet so essential, the process must be such as to throw the colored man under every possible quickening influence. Hence it is not best to separate him carefully from his white brother, and to raise him in an institution by himself, like a tender plant in a hothouse. He needs the contact with the more advanced race. The acknowledgment of his manhood thus given will add to his self-respect, and will fire his nobler ambitions, while the white man will be essentially benefitted by laying aside his unrepublican and unchristian caste-feeling, and coming into sympathy with Burns's immortal declaration, which is true as regards the color of the skin, as well as of poverty, that

"A man 's a man for a' that!"

Colored youth educated wholly apart from the whites lose the stimulus of the competition which they need to have; for it is well known that the progress of a scholar depends upon his classmates as well as upon his teacher. An eager, industrious, ambitious, and able class will tone up every mind which is in it, while a set of dull, apathetic, slothful students will hang as a dead weight upon each individual associated with them. Hence it is not so important to have institutions of learning expressly for the colored race, as it is to have those which are open to them on equal terms with others. And such is the true character of Howard University, the charter of which makes no allusion to race or color, but simply says that there "is hereby established, in the District of Columbia, a University for the education of youth in the liberal arts and sciences, under the name, style, and title of 'Howard University.'" There is therefore no charter-hindrance to its developing into a truly grand National University, filled with students from all parts of our widely-extended country, and drawn from all the races which compose its varied population. For when the United States made over to the University property of great value, the Trustees properly pledged the institution never to make any distinction, in its treatment of students, based upon race, color, or previous condition of bondage. It can never, therefore, proscribe a man because he is white, or because he is black; because he was descended from Shem, or from Ham, or from Japheth; because he was born a king or a slave. And already not a few students of Anglo-Saxon blood have availed themselves of its privileges, while the North American Indian, the Chinese, the South American, and the Greek have here joined the Negro in the zealous pursuit of knowledge. In one department (the Medical) for several years the majority of the students have been white. By such a proper recognition of the colored man in the higher branches of learning, and his consequent necessity of competition with those whom he aspires to equal, there will be secured for him a rapid elevation in intellect and character.

Every case which is at all parallel, confirms the validity of our reasoning. The classical scholar will, perhaps, remember that Cicero, in writing to one of his friends, advises him, when he has occasion to purchase a slave, not to buy one of those stupid Britons. Doubtless, after the Roman wars in Britain, thousands of captives had been sent to Italy and exposed for sale, according to ancient custom; and those who bought them had learned that they were intellectually inferior to slaves obtained from other sources. Why does a Briton no longer bear such a reputation? Because generations of favorable influences have brought him out of the barbaric condition in which he then was, and have educated him into the representative of civilization. Take the case of the Jew, who, in the middle ages, and even till within a century, was regarded with universal odium throughout christendom, was excluded from society, was compelled to live in a separate part of every European city, and was insulted on the street with impunity by any vulgar ruffian. Why has he now almost universal recognition, on an equality with his Gentile brethren? Because he has not only acquired wealth, but has displayed ability in every department of human achievement; because he has furnished Europe with leaders in philosophy, in history, in philology, in statesmanship, and in arts. A modified illustration may even be drawn from the feelings entertained towards certain classes of immigrants in this country. In every land a foreigner is viewed with a measure of disfavor; but for a long time the American popular feeling was one of special aversion towards the immigrant Irish and Germans. The mass of them were of the lower classes, and in their poverty, coarseness, and ignorance seemed below the average American. But since the educated classes have arrived, and since the children of the earlier comers have been to the common schools, and have risen, in many cases, to wealth and to political position, the current of opinion and feeling has rapidly changed, and one less often hears contemptuous references to "the Irish" and "the Dutch." There can be no reasonable doubt, then, that educational forces, rightly brought to bear upon the colored people, will in time work a change in the matter of prejudice; which is only partially an incident of difference of feature and complexion, and is principally a manifestation of caste-pride.

And here the privileges of a university-training will show marked results, not only in individuals, but also in the general mass. For, in order to such a result, all classes of men need appropriate leaders, who shall honorably represent them before others, and who, possessing their confidence, shall wisely guide their aims and efforts in every department of action. The mass of men must and will have leaders. They are gregarious by instinct, and they have not the intelligence to judge and act independently. The ignorant become the victims of ambitious, self-sufficient and incompetent, even if well-meaning leaders. It is the case of the blind leading the blind, with the proverbial result. They also fall an easy prey to designing and hypocritical demagogues, who flatter their vanity, work upon their fears, feed their hopes, appeal to their unenlightened prejudices, and use them as tools with which to work out personal and selfish ends. He must have been a superficial student of human nature in general, and an unsophisticated admirer of negro character in particular, who can persuade himself that the ignorant and unexperienced freedmen of our Southern States have not suffered extensively in these very ways. Only a perpetual miracle could have preserved them. Beyond question they have often been deceived and led astray, religiously and politically, by white men and by those of their own race, who abused their confidence. It is no more certain that emancipation carried to the South a large body of self-denying Christians and philanthropists, anxious to instruct and elevate the freedmen, and who had their true interests at heart, than it is that there went thither also ambitious and unscrupulous adventurers, who cared for the colored race only as some northern politicians care for the Irish, courting them to obtain their votes and to use them as tools for selfish and corrupt ends. It is this fact, with its natural results, which occasions such a malignant utterance as that which the newspapers ascribe to Mr. Toombs, of Georgia, who is represented as recently saying of the colored people:

"They are to be governed as every race of paupers are governed—by those who own the property and give them bread, and just the same as the red man is governed. No inferior man, no man without civilization, has a chance in this race, and I want to save this people from their worst fortunes in the contest. As his friends tried to control him by force and by fraud, we will control him by fraud and force, to prevent him from bringing ruin to us."

If the colored people remain in ignorance, poverty, and degradation, and thus become the natural prey of false friends and open enemies, what can prevent the sentiment of Mr. Toombs from becoming general? The only certain corrective for this evil is general and special education, which shall raise the average intelligence of the masses, so as to make them more capable and independent in their judgments of men and measures, and which shall also provide appropriate leaders worthy of their confidence from among themselves. These leaders must be such as naturally come to the front in organized and cultivated society—the men in all professions and pursuits who to native talent add superior education. There must be a speedy addition of cultivated mind to the colored population if it is to be saved from follies which will be fatal. That grade of mind must operate not only directly and purposely through public addresses and by the press, but in all those quiet, incidental, and unconscious ways of daily and hourly intercourse, which are equally or even more effective. Hence we must have colored lawyers, physicians, editors, authors, clergymen, artists, statesmen, and teachers, whose attainments shall be equal to those of white men in similar occupations, and whose expressed opinions shall have just weight with their race on the various mooted questions which may arise in Church and State.

But, as the Theological Department of our University emphatically intimates, we include the religious among the most powerful and necessary of the educational forces needed to elevate a depressed race. And herein is our advantage over any university supported and controlled by the civil State; which is not only precluded from having a department of theology, but is much fettered in its attempt to recognize and use the Christian religion. Howard University seeks to imbue its students with the principles of the gospel, and to surround them continually with a Christian atmosphere; believing that there can be no genuine success which does not include character, and that there is no such power to regenerate character as the gospel of Jesus Christ. Nothing else so purifies the motives as well as the life, presents so high an ideal, and develops such a sense of responsibility for making the most of a man, for his own sake and that of the world. We attach a special importance to the Theological Department, therefore, because the colored people need an educated ministry, to deliver them from degrading superstitions, to preserve the more intelligent from the errors of infidelity, and to furnish all their communities with those who shall favor genuine progress in whatever tends to the elevation of their race. As the institution receives aid and students from all denominations of Protestant Christians, this department is conducted in the way of genuine catholicity. Four denominations are represented in its Faculty, and it is under the special supervision and care of the Presbytery of Washington and the American Missionary Association at New York, who unitedly provide the instructions and the pecuniary support. Prominence will be given, in the instruction, principally to the doctrines common to evangelical Christianity, rather than to the peculiar tenets of the rival sects; which latter are viewed historically and descriptively rather than for polemic purposes. Here the friends of the freedmen may unite on a broad Christian ground, above the contentions of party zealots, to secure for the best minds a liberal training which yet shall be true to the positive teaching of the New Testament. And we lay the greater stress on this feature, because the chief foes of our evangelical faith, at the present time, among the freedmen, as elsewhere, are Romanism and Skepticism; against both of which it becomes Protestant Christians to stand in solid phalanx rather than in divided companies.

It may be appropriate here to state, for the information of the public, that Howard University has now in operation, prepared to receive students, these several departments:

I. The Academic, which includes five courses of study, from that of the elementary English branches to the usual Classical College Course.

II. The Medical, with a large and finely equipped building, a connected hospital of three hundred beds, and an able faculty—a department having so many professional advantages, that the majority of its students are usually white, and the numbers are continually increasing.

III. The LEGAL. This was last year temporarily discontinued, owing to various difficulties, personal and pecuniary; but it has been reopened this autumn on a small scale, and with hopeful indications for the future.

IV. The THEOLOGICAL, of which I have already spoken, and where may be found a goodly company of pious men, usually of quite mature age, some of whom are already preachers in their own denominations, and whose previous advantages have been very small, but who desire to gain what additional knowledge they may, to fit them to be the religious teachers of their race. With their meager previous preparation we cannot usually carry them through as high and thorough a course as we could desire, but we aim to do good work with them so far as their limited time and training will allow.

Through divine favor, the generous and enlightened action of the United States Government, and the liberality of the Christian public, Howard University has been furnished with spacious grounds and numerous buildings, costing over half a million of dollars, ample for its purposes for years to come, and which not inelegantly crown their commanding site, whence the eye takes in a prospect of peculiar beauty, including the entire city of Washington. There are, besides, valuable vacant lands, adjoining and in other parts of the city, from the sale of which the University hopes eventually to secure partial endowments, but which, in these times of depression, cannot be put upon the market. Its productive property affords but a small income, insufficient to pay the current expenses on their present restricted scale, and requiring to be liberally supplemented by the gifts of the friends of the institution. It has also no permanent scholarships for the aid of indigent students, but is compelled to rely, for this purpose, upon the annual contributions of the charitable. Yet it will be seen that such broad and deep foundations have been laid, as to make it safe and wise for the benevolent and patriotic to build largely upon them in the future. It was the misfortune of the University to commence when the country was in the intoxication of supposed wealth, when large plans were laid and corresponding expenses were incurred, when not only was the present used, but also the future was discounted, and debts were everywhere the order of the day; and also when the enthusiasm for the elevation of the negro was at its height, immediately upon the close of the war. It has consequently shared in the reverses of the times, while a partial reaction has taken place in the feelings of the North with respect to the freedmen, and it has had also the internal changes of administration which accompany fluctuating fortunes. But its friends now feel that the tide is to turn once more in its favor. The floating debt of over one hundred thousand dollars, of three years since, has been entirely discharged, and the only permanent debt on its valuable property is one of eleven thousand dollars. There is reason to believe that it will soon begin to share in the large benefactions of living philanthropists and Christians, and that it will be liberally remembered in the wills of those who may be desirous of leaving behind, at their death, a perpetual fountain of blessing for coming generations.

In closing, the speaker may be permitted a few words personal to himself. In the latter part of a life which has always devoted a large share of thought and action to the welfare of the colored race, he finds himself called, in the providence of God, to preside over the interests of this rising and important institution, of whose object and resources he has been speaking. He is conscious how inadequate are his powers and various attainments to the full discharge of the duties of this position, and it is therefore with humility rather than with pride that he enters upon them. His trust is in the kind indulgence and active cooperation of those who shall be associated with him in the various departments of instruction and in the Board of Trustees, while above all he would crave the blessing of that God whose is all truth, in every department of learning; who delights in the progress of his rational creatures in knowledge and holiness; who is ruling this world in the interests of the kingdom of his Son, Jesus Christ; who, for some great purpose, has brought out of bondage the millions of the freedmen; and who, for a coincident end has established Howard University!

www.ingramcontent.com/pod-product-compliance
Lightning Source LLC
LaVergne TN
LVHW020635110826
845149LV00004B/1202
* 9 7 8 1 4 1 8 1 9 1 1 2 2 *